Sandcastles in the Rain

Lauren Bronwyn Wagner

BookLeaf Publishing

Presentation by *BookLeaf Publishing*

Web: www.bookleafpub.com

E-mail: info@bookleafpub.com

ISBN: 978-93-5761-208-1

First edition 2022

Dedicated to the souls who feel deeply, yet still
shine their light so others can see their way
through the dark.

You are loved.

ACKNOWLEDGEMENT

To everyone who has believed in me from the start. To the ones who have picked me up. To the ones who have given me courage and strength when doubt crept in. I love you.

Marc Webber
Myrtle
Natalie
Laurence
Erin
Matthew
Robert
Joseph
Marc
Darryl
Marion
Waggy
Melissa
Rebecca
Tash
Terry
Peter
Phil
Lynn
Sharyn

PREFACE

These poems were written by Lauren Bronwyn Wagner to explore human connection and all the emotions that come along with that. She aims to open the heart and mind and it is Lauren's hope that her words bring clarity and peace to the reader.

If I'm Anything Lately

Here I am, if I'm anything lately, it's yours
Bewildered, I give all but my flaws
I don't think you could take it all
I remind myself before I fall

Did I let you through my skin?
Did I not realize until you had already sunk in?
Where do you go when the thoughts take hold?
When you fear you're on the verge of losing
control?

Did I let you settle in?
You made a home in my soul and let your life
begin
Did I make the transition easy for your heart
To take shelter from the terrors that were tearing
it apart?

Well here I am
If I'm anything lately
It's yours

Truth

I imagine truth as pearlescent
Like when sun rays shine through a window

I imagine truth as circumstantial
Like how you need light to cast shadow

I imagine truth as buoyant
Like the salty water of the sea

I imagine truth as heroic
Like the boy scared of the hero he could be

I imagine truth as indifferent
Like you could take it or leave it and truth it
would be

I imagine truth as faith
Like you don't have to see it to believe

Come To Me

Come to me in silence
When the dreams begin on a mountain edge
Come to me with an open soul
Streaming sunbeams from your anxious head
Come to me when the shadows play
With echoes that fall off your tongue
Come to me with your frail heart
And I will fight beside you until the war is won

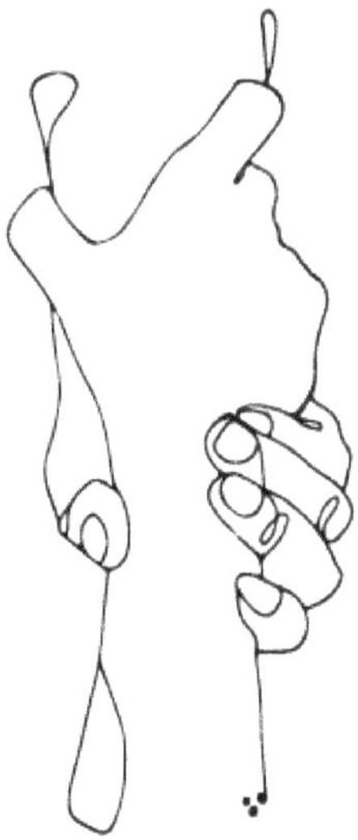

Only You

The stars weren't around then
- there was only you
Hazel eyes, emerald flecks, sprinkling of gold
The warmth that emanated from you was
tangerine and bold
Twinkling of expression
- a cheshire cat grin
Inside you hold natures saccharine

The stars weren't around then
- there was only you
Flushed cheeks and crimson lips
on a bed of moonlit skin

Warrior

She wore her heart on her sleeve
Made of lilac flowers and velvet lace
Everytime it broke open
A portion of her was replaced
- With gilded wings of warriors
And arrows tipped with Oleander
She stood staunch against a jaded world
- Determined not to let it change her

There You Weren't

And there you were, and there you weren't
Dancing on the edge of existence
Faltering, just as you caught up with it

So there you stood, before you fell
Oh how the mighty have fallen
When victory was meant to be a sure thing

Once adored, before quickly forgotten
Now your name barely breaks the silence
Since love has wiped out the internal violence

And there you were, and there you weren't
Dancing on the edge of existence,
Faltering, just as you caught up with it

Your Soul

Make your soul beautiful
Then go out into the world
Make your soul humble
Then go out and heal the hurt
Make your soul luminescent
Then go out and be the light
Make your soul heroic
Then go out and save a life

For You

I whispered quietly to the weeping trees
To carry you kindness from the fallen leaves
I asked for treasures to flower as hope
And grow from your garden on days you
couldn't cope
I ensured all thoughts came from a place of love
So even if I wasn't there, you would know you
were thought of
I requested with gratitude and a humble heart
That in darkness you'd find embers to light a
spark
I sang from my soul a quirky little tune
As thanks to the universe for looking out for you

I said a little prayer for your life to be sweet
Did you do the same for me?

Borrowed Time

Don't send me echoes
With blanched corners
With singed sides
Don't send me incomplete truths
When you know they are lies
Don't send me fragments
With sharp edges
With jagged lines
Don't send me versions of yourself
Hoping one will win the prize
Don't send me excuses
With cloudy judgment
With mottled eyes
Don't send me conditional love
Thinking that I'll take the line
Don't send me the hook
With no bait
With no shine
Don't send me moments for reflection
Darling, we're living on borrowed time

Brother

If I could heal all your emotional scars
I'd rip them from your psyche, bottle them into
jars
I'd break down the barricades set up in your
mind
The ones you have locked up over time
If I could take your tears from every time you've
cried
In a heartbeat I'd do it and wear them with pride
If I could carry your anguish so your soul only
knew peace
Without a doubt brother, your demons would
already be with me

Diamonds

There's diamonds in you
I caught flashes of them in your eyes
Beneath the broken surface
And your murky mirror of disguise
There's diamonds all through you
Hidden in corners of your mind
An ode to old heartbreaks
And memories left behind

My Friend

You give from yourself as if you are a never
ending vessel of love and hope
Taking on others problems, when it becomes too
much for them to cope
Never expecting a single thing in return
There is alot from you that we could learn

You carry the world on your shoulders all with
dignity and poise
Marching through the chaos to bring silence to
the world's noise
You've witnessed so much turmoil but refuse to
let it dim your light
Continuously shining like a beacon, for hurting
souls in the night

I could write a thousand lines and it would never
be enough
To thank you my friend, for your never ending
love

On Top of The World

I sat on top of the world
Grasping at souls to release the hurt
While shadows danced and divvied up the time
I lost control of yours before it became mine
You faltered, you floundered, you dissolved a
mountain of lies
I sat watching, but you did not look at me this
time

I sat on top of the world
Experiencing unmeasurable hurt
While you played the jester one step out of time
I gave you yours, before you could take mine
You flourished, you favoured, you absolved
every hand written rhyme
I sat, unable to conjure up another single line
Because you couldn't see me this time

I sat on top of the world
Not quite as sacred as all the other girls
While you romanced the whole of humankind
They gave you theirs, but you still didn't have
mine
You fancied, you fascinated, you forbode anyone
wanting to shine

I sat, glistening - as you turned your head to the side
A second earlier and you could have seen me this time

If You Could See Inside

I loved fearlessly
And he was strong
Like black coffee with a dash of whiskey
But beneath that he was soft

If you could see inside

He was rough, like loose gravel roads
Like the back roads that lead to home
But he was quiet in his mind

If you could see inside

He danced with the darkness
That chased daylight away
Before the moon could rise
But his glow within was bright

If you could see inside

He was a gracious liar
Like the calm before the storm
A silken web of lies
But truth was all he left behind

If you could have seen inside

The Other Side

I will hold you
Through memories kept in my mind
Through words woven onto my soul
With the gilded markers of time

I will hold you
In the quiet moments of life
When the dreams that haunt me
Sing lullabies throughout the night

I will hold you
When the moon is brightest in the sky
And the stars flicker and dance
As you meander through your maze of goodbyes

I will hold you
As the waves crash and change with the tide
And I will speak to you in whispers
Until we meet on the other side

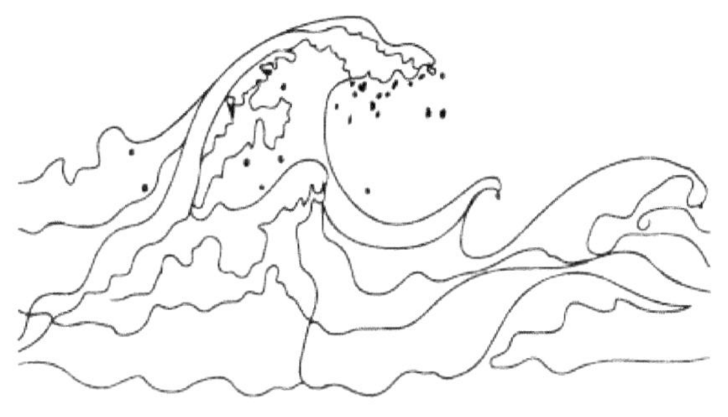

Fortune Favours The Brave

It was said in a way designed to encourage
Designed to discourage fear
Words spoken by heroes
Heroes that are no longer here

Perhaps it's wise to be a gentleman
Even when others are not
The wisdom that you echoed
Time has not forgot

It was suggested that the Brave win
That through trials they succeed
But the fortune that most favoured
Was never part of your creed

Your faith wasn't learned in Church
You didn't read about virtue from a book
But when the rogue waves crashed
Natures miracles were not overlooked

It's expected for time to march on
As if the world is still the same
Your voice is no longer heard
But the lessons you taught remain

Through the music and the banter

And all the love your soul gave
I hope we'll meet again one day
If Fortune favours the brave

I Am

I am art, I am the shiver you get when music
plays
I am vodka, I am the crutch you need to pass the
days
I am vocal, but I keep my opinions quiet anyway
I am clean, but it doesn't mean you won't see my
house in disarray

I am love, I am the Ace of Cups
I am hope, I am the one who doesn't give up
I am highly strung, but I won't wind you up
I am truth, but probably not the one you want to
bring up

I am empathy, I am compassion when
compassion needs
I am anxious, I am what anxiety feeds
I am broken, but I'm clearing out the weeds
I am bad, but the good by far exceeds

Society's Echo

She was gold dust bedewed by rain
She was mesmerising enchantment
Cursed by shame and pain
She let her mind run rampant
With echoes of former flames
For those who knew, she was romantic
While others mused disdain
Perhaps she was even a little frantic
But I'm told the song remains the same
She said her nightmares were implanted
As if to shift the blame
And by morning her words were recanted
While she camouflaged to play the game
As if society only rewards advancement
So long as it's all the same

My Teeth Used To Fit Together

I remember my mouth was full
My head had thoughts that filled it
I ached for moments
I'd get lost under the back stairs
Where skin met dirt and I had the naivety to
pretend I didn't hurt
The whites of my eyes were that
And the sparkle existed
Obnoxiously
Like it couldn't help but shine
As if it was purely... mine

Back when my teeth used to fit together

I Wonder

When I was younger I was too caught up in the
here and now
To worry too much about the future
And now all I do is think about the future
I don't appreciate the here and now

So I wonder where is the in-between?
Of the life I've lived and the life yet to be seen
And I wonder what they'll make of me
When my bones become bleached and my soul
has long departed me
If all the electrons firing in my head are going to
fade out
I wonder then, what all these thoughts were
about?
And if the ache inside my chest fades to black
What happens with all these feelings I held
back?
If my journey here ends when my breath is no
more

I wonder then, what came before?

Youth

There is beauty in the youthful mind
Seasons pass slowly, conversations are one of a
kind
A single moment can become an eternity
While you hesitate between lust and uncertainty

www.ingramcontent.com/pod-product-compliance
Lightning Source LLC
LaVergne TN
LVHW021312200726
843509LV00012B/1889